[MUG-yar-az-knee]

['Make it Hungarian']

Magyarázni

Helen Hajnoczky

Coach House Books, Toronto

Published with the generous assistance of the Canada Council for the Arts and the Ontario Arts Council. Coach House Books also acknowledges the support of the Government of Canada through the Canada Book Fund and the Government of Ontario through the Ontario Book Publishing Tax Credit.

LIBRARY AND ARCHIVES CANADA CATALOGUING IN PUBLICATION

Hajnoczky, Helen, author
     Magyarázni / Helen Hajnoczky. -- First edition.

Poems.
Issued in print and electronic formats.
ISBN 978-1-55245-327-8 (paperback)

     I. Title.

PS8615A3857M34 2016   C811'.6   C2015-908210-2

Magyarázni is available as an ebook: ISBN 978 1 77056 441 1 (EPUB), 978 1 77056 442-8 (PDF), 978 1 77056 457 2 (MOBI)

Purchase of the print version of this book entitles you to a free digital copy. To claim your ebook of this title, please email sales@chbooks.com with proof of purchase or visit chbooks.com/digital. (Coach House Books reserves the right to terminate the free digital download offer at any time.)

I am a word
in a foreign language
  – Margaret Atwood, *The Journals of Susanna Moodie*

My hovercraft is full of eels.
                  – 'Dirty Hungarian Phrasebook,'
                    Monty Python's Flying Circus

Save me your space-age techno-babble, Attila the Hun.
                  – Zack Brannigan, *Futurama*

Diddynek
[For my father]

Pronunciation Guide

Bad, as an extended cat, as by absence, etc.
Like a tsunami, check your cheek like an etching.
The wide deck, like when you were a kid playing.
Jam in the fridge, the edge of a bridge.
You like less, on the edge of the bed.

You write a cheque, the same but without.
In a café you find euphoria.
Get on your legs, you go, etc. (Not used in English)
Similar to speaking like here, not so in English.
Basically, you say hi, but you're behind and mute.
Human thick and thin.

You could lead, or leave sow seeds.
Swim in the sea. Yes, you have faith, the key.
Kiss, you're weak, make lists, you leave.
Hey, your mind might assume a lying thing.
(Anywhere else), knit bones.

You go, the snow, forced sorcery.
(Not used in English; corresponds to the German Ö).
(Not used in English; a longer, more closed variant of Ö).
Your hands numb now from overuse.

You buy peas, apricots, you can hope.
You can wish it, say it, share it, shout it.
At least you can tell, or estimate.
Feast on something similar to stew.
(Not used in English) rude fool.

(Not used in English, corresponds to the german Ü).
(Not used in English) from every view, you could evolve.
Your room, clean, vacuumed.
you leave behind roses.
Pleasure, leisure, genre.
Deserted.

Altatódal

Doll, this altitude
holds the night close to the dull moon.
But here, gleaming like pitch,
we're home again.

In English: peace attends the breeze.
Angels watch you tumble from the trees,
swaddled in nightlight,
aching for daybreak.

In Hungarian: the peppers and carrots
and onions take up flutes and fiddles,
flailing stalks and jiving roots,
they leap into the pot.

Instead of waiting for your branch to break,
you're ebbed to sleep by a simmering cauldron,
the English of your mother's song,
Hungarian of your father's.

The nightlight dances on the wall
like a pepper set for the soup.
All to tell, not too dull.
You sleep.

A

Állatkert

A K-car or school bus or Suburban to tour the
living bestiary of the plains. Point and this is
the North American land-dwelling water horse,
the mountains, cold north, snow, and each hide
is a map splotched with continents, aerial views of
possible worlds where a cow is a hippo, where a
hippo is a horse, where Hungarian is Latin, where
the Suburban is broken down at the Petro-Can just
outside of town, bus broken down in the Kananaskis,
K-car stuck in the city snow. Black squirrels
scramble up birch trees, cows graze, a field
of hay bales a bowl of giant Shredded Wheat and
the time rolls by, foothills roll into Rockies, snow
settles, packs into ice on the sidewalk. You are
a quiet little creature, snow mammal,
prairie dweller, adapted from a temperate
climate, the rhythm of your hibernation,
the Latin of your silly jokes.

Belváros

You wait, this charming place,
       luminous towers,
     columns of bells,
  chimes that scrape the evening sky.

The inner city, sunset,
     sheer walls of light reverberate
with all the tones and glow
     of your resentment, this place.

You have hated the
    wash of lustrous peach,
       you have missed the
     tinted clouds, the swell of
             incandescent night.

The gong of evening
      shimmers, clanging chorus of
traffic signals, sprong of fluorescent
         signs in the twilight.

The glint of your reflection that
    rings off the ground-floor windows,
alone you wait, cozy in
    the awning of dusk
       lilting from the buildings.

Sharp clang of memory.
Twinkle of memory.
Chime of the city.

B

Cukorka

Your reflection
        splintered in foil
these solemn treats

            this bitter history
sugary sweet

unhooked from the tree
                you melt

a plastic angel dipped
            in flames, blurred
    and bubbling

you unwrap
the old world
        you chew
                and smile

        you don't swallow
    until they look away.

Cserkészek

Check if you're ready
Roll and tighten your neckerchief
Roll on your stockings, stand at attention

Deliver your lines with conviction
A more personable person
A more magyar Hungarian

Paint eggs, throw rosewater
Thread needles, weave leather
Serve dinner to your elders

Recite your practised lines
With your flawless intonation
With your perfect lack of understanding

How well you know your friends
Whom you cannot understand
Who cannot understand you

Savour the illicit snippets of English
Smuggled out to the parking lot
Together you roll and ignite secrets

Duna

The river flows clear or muddy
you know the river flows cold
or warm or

The river cuts across countries
or it springs locally and
ambles through every city or

The river is shallow enough to wade or
deep enough to drown in, the bed
scattered with bombed-out bridges or

The iron was hauled back up on land
you know the river ribbons
the countryside or you know

The river slices through the city, one bank
heaved up like a tidal wave, one bank
spread out like a flood plain or

You knew the river's name
before or you
didn't know the river at all.

No common contemporary word

Sputtering drone, petticoats,
    embroidered vests,
  red leather boots.

No one cooks over an open fire,
    scratches words into wood,
      drinks by candlelight.

You want a sharp consonant,
    an axe of a word to split myths,
to cleave false memories.

    You want a word to spit
this was no world, no time
    anyone lived in.

The truth was a city,
baroque façades, paved streets,
three-piece suits and hatpins.

But war is a dry husk
  to jam in people's mouths,
    so you'll let the letter rust and dull.

(The rhythm of that drone,
that twirl of skirts,
the burn of liquor in your throat.)

Dzsúsz

Every drop, this
        vocabulary
   squeezed to the rind,

these letters,
        down to the pith,
this pulpy language,
        sugary thick.

You thirst for something
smooth, something that flows,
a cool rinse, bright
and clear.

Watered down, no need to sip,
        you can slug it back,
           past your lips.

Swallow the meaning,
diluted,
it slips down easy.

Elfelejt

Away, half, yet you still
   grasp, get out of the car,
get up, the railing. Where
  once you, but now only, you
     leave the party to go dancing,
you step out into the early
  morning air, the breeze
     whirling the skirt of your
nightgown, the dew beneath
  your, yet then around you follow,
     in circles, you are after or being
followed. No more, your hand or,
  could you make out, what
     days, no more language but
that gingerbread man so cute
  with the icing and sprinkles
     how could you not laugh.
You won't remember this but,
     long after you forgot, still the
candles huddled in the church,
     empty pews echoing your
                 children's sobs.

Ég

Gather kindling to build your
tiny pyre. When sunset cooks down
to its embers, set a match to the
mess of sticks, watch the bark stutter,
hissing sparks into the firmament.

The night ablaze, your dreams a mess
of ash and coal, you settle down by the
fire, the flames, ashes of accents,
spitting broken words.

The pink tingle of dawn, a pot of water
over the fire, you wake punctuated with dew,
illuminated with evergreen air,
the morning air more crisp more true
than the bramble of your cursive.

A yawn has no language but the heat
from your body curling in the cold air.

Forradalom

For a song, your song, your
    sweet soft face the day you
were born. Here, only because
      the gloom loomed too heavy
there. You, old enough now to play
    with the fancy dolls, their
      scarlet slippers, the pompoms
of their tiny headdresses.
    Don't forget what they suffered,
what they sacrificed for you.
    But you, so you should fall asleep
with a sad song in your heart,
    should never put away your toys,
      no matter how old you grow.
Whether you're twirling the pleats of
    your skirts at the dance house or
running to the bank; whether
  you're stewing gulyás or browsing
    at the mall; whether you're
memorizing folksongs or sipping
    tea, watching the rain from the
kitchen window, remember to feel
    the weight of every happiness
      crushing you like hail.
Every happiness you have
is an accident of war.

Gépel

The specimen of the electric typewriter gaping
on the kitchen table on which you
sit cross-legged, leaning over your subject,
your instructor hands you his
pliers and wrenches, helps you when your
small fingers, purpled and slippery
like plum dumplings, can't pry the keys
from the hammers. Your hair tied back,
you snip wires as your instructor offers
tips in a language the machine couldn't
accommodate.

The era of analogue dissection passed, you are
now the sought-after expert on
digital vivisection, called on to
give teleconferences, lectures on logging into
email accounts, hooking up printers. The
pulsing machine now ready with the Unicode
for all required accents, but the character palette
too difficult to explain in anything but
English. Your instructor now puzzled
by the specimen on the table, you lean over and
cut and paste it for him.

Gyógyul

Gurgle of pneumonia,
saltwater gargle.

You can't sleep,
grip rum and hack.

Throat glowing,
groan of nascent ash.

Wipe the fever
from your hands.

You'll feel better with a warm
towel soaked in vinegar

wrapped around your
neck.

Bite of caraway, the soup
swells and boils to soothe

your hateful lung,
your throat will heal.

Do you feel better, little quiche?
Honey, have some tea.

Himnusz

Is then all more
frozen heart.
You coddled, bundled
should you fall.
Vengeful heart, hand
cramped, shrug it off.
Bawl, shorn kite
ragged taste.
Horizon the rain
vague estranged.
Maybe holding
marred and narrow?
A mutilated shame
you doze.

Stand by you blessed
good care, buoyancy.
To uplift you in
armoured arms.
If you should wade
into the fray.
Long ripped apart
by ill fate.
You ache for a time of
calm relief.
Wail: have you not
burned for your sins?
Your past affronts and
future wrongs.

Idő

Say you want to understand
time as a construct, or say
you need to know
the weather report, or
you can lament how quickly a
sunny day runs out, or you can
marvel at how long the rain lasts.

When it snows, you know to
hide inside, you notice
each year crashing by,
house ticking with
thunder, but decades
drift by on a soft wind.

There will always be time for
sunshowers, for sunburns,
time to exaggerate the cold.

Check the weather report,
set your clocks,
and go to sleep.

You have the time to wake, slowly,
put on the coffee,
watch dawn meander
through the east-facing windows
while everyone else is
fast asleep.

I

Írástudatlanság

You languish in this land,
fertile mud of willows and slop;
your nails sown with dirt,
irate, your studies stuck.

Your palms won't
bloom; no letters, but caught
in your throat, you can
read your heart so well.

The pen tip dull when you
roll it across your mute page, sharp
when you roll it on
your tongue.

You're an applied student,
you can sketch your
ignorance so well with your
fallow fingers; blot of dumb.

You plant your pen in the muck,
wait for the seeds to sprout and
twine around the stake, wait for your
letters to bloom , to go to seed.

Jelentés

Yell at you not yet not
  you're not yelling not yet
not to tell how to tell this
  to just say it you'd let it be
but before you say anything
  before you see what's said
  you scream it before you
regret it you'll let it go before
  you are not yelling you are
    you just said that you said
that you see what you are
  yelling before you see you
scream it not to add to not
  to you too and before you
say something you come in
    before you yell anything
not to hit this note not to
  point this out not to grind
this down and you've been
  here before but you forget
      the reason.

Konyhanyelv

In a separate bowl add a
pinch and sauté, add and
simmer until

To taste if desired,
if necessary,
if desired until

Form until flat, fold in
with a spoon, fluff
with a fork

Cook through until
firm, fry until
crisp, bake until soft

Serve with and add to
good with
if desired

Spilled on the floor, a slip
of the tongue, beaters
against the bowl

You add too much,
your palate parched,
you burn your tongue

A crusted pot,
a clutter of cutlery,
dishwasher stuffed.

You cooked this up, your hunger,
your sweetness, alone in the
kitchen, you lick the spoon.

Lángos

Languid bowl of mashed potatoes, flour burnt
to the side of the fryer.

You: long for something familiar. Street food in
wax paper for your forints, here you're the cook
collecting loonies from the wicket in the church
basement.

Or you: attend the service once a month and
you look forward to the carafe of coffee, the
chocolate and strawberry wafers, warm bread,
oil soaking through the paper towel, garlic powder,
you pretend to understand the chatter, you
spill salt on the table, on the linoleum floor, you
wipe your hands on your Sunday skirt.

Lyuk

Oh look, you tangled
your embroidery again

Snarled loops of pink and violet
crimped and knotted

You deftly split the fibres
as you jam the thread

Blunt on the needle you
puncture the linen

Everywhere but the stencil
you are the undisputed expert

Of sticking your sore fingers
trying to correct this

Mess of thread this lumpy
flower you are

Never going to sew anything
as good as your grandmother.

Mulhey

This place to build a better place.

Collected from the grinder,
a steel drum full of
fairy dust you toss
across the shop yard.

Low grey buildings, smokestacks and grain elevators,
styrofoam container of fried rice
from the crummy Irish pub
at the edge of the industrial park.

Hoppy cloud spewing from the
brewery, you poke around the old motorcycles,
you learn to weld, you set off on an
expedition through the wild of rusted machines,
abandoned lean-tos of pipes and siding,
every nook a hook for your imagination.

But you grew up and you
Work inside you are
Never tired you are
Always tired you are
Never tanned you have
Soft sore hands.

You haven't built anything.

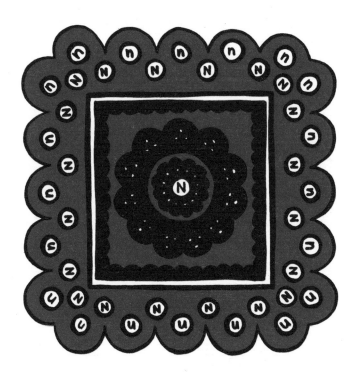

Nem

No, Hungarian is not a gendered language,
but no, you do not want to play Joseph in the
goddamned Christmas play again this year!

No, you're not jealous that no one asks her which
bathroom key she wants, even though
you've been asked this while wearing a skirt.

No, no long hair, no stockings,
no heels, no tailored shirts. No way to indicate
them, no not them, not her, not him, just them.

No, she always gets to play Mary, and no,
you do not want to play a goddamned
shepherd either!

Just no.

Nyugat

Before you north, south at your back,
        to your left the sun dozes off,
                and to your right it wakes.

You are healing, not a heliocentrist,
        you are planted in the middle, you are
a seed in the permafrost you are

you, or you are the centre of this
        narrative, geocentrist, east depends on
where you are still, or on this non-continent,
      or spinning still, but the west, anyway, has
        proven calm.

as you heal, still centred,
lay your head down.

Otthon

You are meant to inherit this
    rococo ache. Delicate little
        cakes and spoons, home torn away.

    But your city is an ice pick, razor
horizon, glass skyscrapers, mountain
        river, shards of ice.

You adopted another's resentments,
an excuse to escape
the clean prairie lines of home.

Now, in your own chosen exile,
    you have your own ache,
bright winter, displaced.

        In your memory where it is now
    always spring,
                cool breeze lingering.

But dreams melt like ice, concrete is
    concrete, your new city, humid,
        thick embrace of summer nights.

            Here, your yearning for the
open sky, there, your
squandered time.

You're coming going leaving
        back again. Home is wherever
                you are not.

Óperencia

Once there was in the land that never was,
Against the seventh sixth country and beyond,
Still beyond the sea, followed once and went,
Now tell this story:

Once, a beautiful day in a meadow,
Once, there was a clearing of that kind,
And it is still there, where it is, not beyond,
Still there, where it never was, and they're
Still alive if they haven't died, they still run if
They haven't stopped, they still sing if
They haven't died, they still walk if they can, and
They still live in happiness if they aren't dead,
And with good fortune, they still live peacefully,
If they haven't died.

This is your story, this is the end, this was true.
The rest goes on this way as well, so this is the end,
And if that's the story, it was told, it has run out,
This was the story, and the end, but if you want,
Run away with it.

They still went on, some direction or other,
Until they stopped.

And this was true once,
In the land
That never was.

Öcsem

You have no interest in alternate timelines. You have no need of patriarchal lineages. You have enough siblings. You are an adventure or travel narrative spinoff series. You are father enough on your own. You love your mother, your wife, your daughters. You are not curious about someone else's future past.

Or, you are from the main timeline, but you have no sympathy for the patriarch. You too launched your own spinoff series set at a slightly later date. You too are father enough on your own. You love your mother, wife, daughters, and son. You are curious about how earlier timelines might have gone.

You aren't looking to add any new characters or you are actively looking for new characters. You stumble upon a clue, or you are hiding clues all over. Either way you meet, your narratives resolved, you are similar, you are different, you are writing a new guest special, you are here now and you are very glad you met.

Őriz

You work the bulbs from the soil,
    chisel the sprouts into stems,
        sweep out the curves of petals,
whittle away the withered leaves,
your winter garden plied to life,
    thriving through the seasons.

Your careful blossoms safe from the
decay of the outdoors, of being
choked out by wild flowers or the
sly perennials.
Bleeding hearts.
Mountain ash.
April frost.

You can appreciate the easy flourish
of local flora
    but continue to coax the
        heirloom seeds with
    watchful eye.
            You sand the delicate soil.

Paradicsom

Glory of sun through
the market stalls' awnings

choir of fruit in the stands

sample slices,
each a glimmering harp

strum of juice on your tongue

bite of knowledge, what this
salad, sauce, stew will taste like

how it should be dressed, this
smooth flesh of bitter vine.

You wander the shop's stacks, dust off
tales of knights driving swords through
shields, tales of shadowy figures in dark
cobblestone alleys sliding daggers through ribs.

You find a pressed rose in the pages of a
fairy tale, the thick flower imprinted on the
pages, you prick yourself on a crisp thorn like a

Stray needle from your Christmas tree in
the rug, stray needle from your sewing box,
stray fish hook in the corner of a drawer,
claw shed by the bookstore's cat.

Enough of dark stores. You stride from the
antiquarian's with a chime, into the sun, you
go home, you clean up after last night's party.
You don't squint pressing a needle into the side
of a fat balloon.

Rák

Your cells raked over the sand,
pinched and filtered,
divided over and over,
until there are too many to count,
like a pile of sand in your shoe.

You wonder where the time went,
why you never got that pet hermit crab,
why you never took pleasure in astrology,
why you never took the time to read
the R section of the dictionary.

You once marvelled at the horizon where
the sea and sky met,
you watched the constellations
fracture on the waves.

But you scuttled away from the world,
you grew a hard shell, you waited
for the stars to align, you waited
to be smashed and roasted
raked over the coals.

Upon reflection,
you've had a good life, a long life.
You won't take this as a sign.
You won't hide this time.
You won't plan your last meal.

But you can't help but feel
the prickle of claws on your skin.
The dread of the tide coming in.

Sírya

Grief is a shorn nerve,
the soggy earth,
a monument
covered in moss.

You were born too late
to appreciate the scale
of pleading against
this decay.

But you appreciate
that you bloomed
from this humus,
this reuse of atoms.

Her maiden name
a lullaby,
sunflower carved
into a headstone.

Your namesake,
you look down
at your own
resting place.

Szotár

So here in exile
      you are stuck in tar.
The viscous decay
holding your vocabulary in place,
     your slang preserved
     in the decomposing sludge.
Your words, stasis, black ooze,
     you cannot move
          but dissolve away.

In the beginning there
was the language and
the language was with
you and the language
was you but

Decrepit, a plume of
     smoke or crumble of burnt
words, compacted, you are
       the skeletal remains, a relic,
anthropological evidence.
     You hang, clinging to
phrases that will disintegrate
when pulled to the surface,
clogged with muck, you cling
to strings of words
too weak to hold your weight,
     too brittle to help you
        heave yourself
           up to the light.

Templom

You do tedium with aplomb
Sit kneel stand sit kneel sit still

Lay language
Opaque as Latin

A warble of old voices
Shimmer of candles

Your vision tingling green
Ears illuminated with static

Made mystic
For lack of fresh air

You count the pieces of stained glass
You flip through the hymnal

You toe the seam of your stocking
Balance the kneeler on your toes

You contemplate the painting
Of mother and child

Enthroned before the Carpathians
Certain there is no such parable

No reading from István's first letter
To the Hungarian-Canadians

T

Tyúk

flutter of rosewater,
        painted eggs

starch-smoothed soups and stews,
      swirl of noodles

           flourish of shavings,
grain of wood through the carving

your feathers, your meaning,
      your sore throat, your pecking

 your metaphor or mother,
the new spring grass sprouts

your cement keep,
      your scrabbling claws

      you flew away, lost your accent,
afraid of your own awkward squawks

tricked by the fox,
 taken in by the wolf

plump cushion of feathers,
      be wary, boastful fowl

77

Udvarló

You are a field
And one day you'll be fair

No matter the shelf
You can pull down the thread

Your sure neck while unpacking books
You learn to impersonate a Scot at customs

You can say love
You can say revolution

That is to say, you can say
You can pull leeks, you can do it for a dollar

But it'll throw you off-kilter
Your first complete phrase

You revolt, you love
A field, a stitch, a horse in water

A way to divide and lick
A flick of the tongue

You're fair.

Útikönyv

Paperback travel guide for a
                    hardcover country.
Signatures of thoroughfares,
                    stitched with streets.
Tipped-in cathedrals, coffee houses.

Appendix of relics:
a. Saint's hand.
b. Garden of Soviet statues.

Each leaf set:
Recto: Prominent structures,
familiar foods, turns of phrase.
Verso: Turns of phrase,
it's changed since the '50s.

Special-edition insert with the
        annotated map showing you
the family home, the church,
the hospital, the school, each fled.

A chapter for the market: colour illustrations
of yellow peppers, paprika, dried sausages.
    A chapter for the hotel room: cleaned and
straightened on departure.

Pockets for pressing: a return
   ticket, baggage stickers. Shelved between
the dictionary and travel journal
        it gathers the dust around it like
            children to a storyteller
                and whispers its secrets.

Ünnepel

Your boot in the window,
    as if a saint might fall for that.
Sweet oranges, dark chocolate,
    a decorative switch, clot of coal.

Shepherded out of the
    house to stare at the stars
after the hum of midnight mass,
    sharp squeak of boots in the snow.

Tree sheltering the undergrowth of gifts.
    The evergreen paper adorned with paisley
        that concealed the dollhouse
    the year the tree fell over during dinner.

Or the year all you wanted
    was to sulk and blame diction.
    Not the season of forgiveness,
this memory glows the hottest.

But fried fish or turkey,
    reusable tinsel, tangle of lights,
    regrets diluted, hope, this song.
        You find joy in this.

Űrt

Atmosphere a mix of
particles that sustain,
particles that corrode, and you
      could blast your way through the
       Kármán line to the
   vacuum beyond, test your
oxygen tank alone in the
  quiet, see how long you can
float free from the context of orbit before
      falling back toward this pull this
   home this plummeting depth this
safety net that entangles you.

Would you, floating alone, reach
  for your intercom, or would you say
    that you miss having someone to talk to,
or would you say you don't
      know what to say,
    engage thrusters and
   shoot away, or would you
      brace for re-entry.

Viszontlátásra

You are here you leave and
come back you
look back through before this you
   used only hello to say

Looking over your back
   you are still greeting until
   again and you are lying
you will leave this home not
   your home you have left
      your own home you have

Just started to settle in before
going back again and you will
again say hello or again and

Be back, that look, the one
      you exchange until again and
        there is no end.

Goodbye until again.

This letter, this
    rift, this fault line along the
continents,
jagged, the magma
            surges,
      a tree smashed to
  cinder, bevelled by
  thunder, lightning strike,
                a crack in the ceiling,
                the water gets in,
                the fire gets in.

And you, foreigner,
    on the other side of this tectonic shift,
        with your foreign tongue you
lick the water
that trickles from the ceiling,
warm your hands on the
smouldering stumps, on the
woods' desecration, you thirst
and shiver.

You wait for
it all to explode.

Arms crossed,
        knock-kneed,
thumbs twiddled,
  your arched fingers
a church steeple.

You follow the map
    under cover of night,
dull thud of shovel
    against wooden box,
      pickaxe and trowel,
earth in your fingernails.

You are ready to cast
  your vote, ready to take
your place on stage.

  You will not strike
    it from your mouth.
You cross your heart.

Yank and wish for a forked tongue,
    a serrated wire of serifs,
        a sharp shard stuck in your teeth.

Two paths diverged in the woods.
One was lined with poison ivy.
The other was lined with poison ivy.

Consonant or vowel, you have no
    patience for arbitrary
        rules, artificial limits, you have
           ambitions.

You would split a
        sternum for the right word. Shred your
  clothes crawling in the mud
      under the barbed-wire fence at the border.

You would pick your teeth with tradition and
    spit out the seeds,
        break the wishbone.
    Belly full of sweet fruit.

Zászlo

Absent fabric as politics, you snip
    your rebellion, you peer into
        the space you're creating,
the gravel at your feet but
      red, white, green, this is
    your dirt.

Red: A soup stain on an
apron, a pile of
leaves, political hue.

White: Freezer-burned prairie, life
encrusted in ice crystals, fog and
freezing shock of illiteracy.

Green: Each little seed that took
in the foreign soil, sun-warmed
shoots and sprigs and buds.

Through the seasons you clip a space for
    your unrest, your nostalgia,
      your misunderstandings.

    Tradition of yearning,
a desecrated flag
    hoisted to half-mast
      in memory of a broken pulley.

Zsibbad

You've been here longer now
than you were ever there and then some.
That old here of home,
a faint outline of a baroque façade,
memory of neighbours' mannerisms,
a grandparent's gestures,
layouts of metro stations,
a muffled feeling of the last day.
You weren't paying attention
to this kind of detail.

You preserved what you picked out,
canned it, you keep the jars up on the shelf,
guard them carefully for special occasions,
though you won't take them down,
though you forget what they taste like,
wouldn't recognize the flavour
if you dipped in a spoon.
Stale now, anyway.

Your hands numbed now from overuse,
yet everything you touch still stings.
Nerves bent and pinched,
wrists pushed and twisted.
Hyperextended.

My tongue, now numb, like a burn
from coffee too soon off the campfire.
You warned me of it too late, my own
hands now atrophied and stinging.
No use for use, with who and how.
I can roll it around in my mind,
but not off the tip of my tongue.
Who could I speak with, but you?
Who would want to?
Why would I?
I can't but I can't.

Zs

Learning Activities

*S*ound it out. Sing me a song. Go for a car ride with your family through southern Alberta. Wait for the Number 6 bus at the corner of 3rd St. and 6th Ave. SW in Calgary, Alberta. Enjoy a piece of szaloncukor. Make friends at Hungarian Scouts. Go for a swim in the Danube. Appreciate an antiquated letter. Use an anglicized word for 'juice.' Try not to think about the tragedy of Alzheimer's. Appreciate the night sky, the campfire burning. Consider the impact of the 1956 Hungarian Revolution on your daily life. Dismantle a typewriter, and then type up a report on your experience of this process. Get well soon! Sing the national anthem of Hungary. Take your time. Learn how to read and write. Try to understand. Speak a common, everyday Hungarian. Enjoy a piece of fried potato bread. Stitch up the holes. Visit your father's welding shop. Just say no. Circle Eastern Europe on a map. Go home for a visit. Watch an episode of *Magyar népmesék* (I recommend *Róka koma*). Find your little brother. Stand watch. Enjoy a tomato while contemplating the nature of heaven. Please note that Q is not a true Hungarian letter. Try not to think about the tragedy of cancer. Visit your grandmother's grave. Read the dictionary. Attend mass at St. Elizabeth of Hungary Church located at 819 13th Ave. SW in Calgary, Alberta. Have a bowl of chicken soup. Have your boyfriend help you unpack your books in your new apartment in Montreal, Quebec, while reading to him from the *Teach Yourself Hungarian* book that accompanies a set of four language lesson CDs. Select a travel guide (I recommend *The DK Eyewitness Budapest Travel Guide*). Celebrate Christmas. Fill the void. Learn a new, complicated, multisyllabic word for 'see you soon.' Please note that W is not a true Hungarian letter. Please note that X is not a true Hungarian letter. Please note that Y is not a true Hungarian letter. Cut the sickle and hammer out of a communist-era Hungarian flag. Tell me, do you miss speaking Hungarian? That is, do you miss your father?

Acknowledgements

Thank you to my parents, Ruth and Steven Hajnoczky, to my sister Julya Hajnoczky and to all the members of my extended family. Thank you to David Tkach for being there every step of the way.

Thank you to all the wonderful people in my life who, each in their own way, helped with this book. Thank you to Mark Abley, Attila Andai, Marianna Andai, Malcolm Bauld, Derek Beaulieu, Kristen Beaulieu, Maddie Beaulieu, Emily Bitting, Christian Bök, Philip Cercone, Jonathan Crago, Dave Crosbie, Jacqui Davis, Kit Dobson, Filomena Falocco, Erin Fortier, Paloma Friedman, Stephen Glasgow, Elena Goranescu, Jack Hannan, Tricia Henry, Jessica Howarth, Kevin Jagernauth, Ian Kinney, Rob Mackie, Kyla Madden, Jacqueline Mason, Susan McIntosh, rob mclennan, Laurel Ovenden, Andrew Pinchefsky, Joanne Pisano, Rachael Pleet, Jennifer Roberts, Ian Sampson, Simon Schreiber, Laura Schultz, Brian Scrivener, Shanna Shadoan, Peter Steiner, Enikő Szép, Nailissa Tanner, Regan Toews, Carmie Vacca, Ryan Van Huijstee, Roy Ward and Denise Williams.

Thank you to Raizelle Aigen, Carina de Klerk, Klara du Plessis, Dean Garlick and Alan Reed, whose advice improved this work.

Thank you to Susan Holbrook for being the most amazing and insightful editor and for everything she did to make this book better. Thank you to Alana Wilcox, Veronica Simmonds, Heidi Waechtler and to all those at Coach House Books for their kind support, their incredibly hard work and for all they've done for me and for this book. Working with them has been an honour and privilege.

Thank you to Oana Avasilichioaei, Derek Beaulieu and Phil Hall for reading the manuscript of this work and for their kind words. Thank you to all the members of the Hungarian-Canadian community in Calgary, who inspired much of this book. Thank you also to the members of the Hungarian-Canadian communities in Western Canada I interviewed in 2012. Their stories, insights and generosity have left an indelible mark on me, and though this book focuses on my own experiences, it is informed by everything I learned from them. Thank you once more to my sister Julya Hajnoczky for accompanying me on the trip as the project's photographer.

Poems from *Magyarázni* have appeared in Rusty Toque (Issue 2, 2012), *filling Station* (Issue 59, 2014), *Poetry* (June 2015) and *Matrix* (Issue 100, 2015). Thank you to each of these publications for including my work.

Thank you to Gary Barwin for interviewing me for *Jacket2* in 2013 as part of his 'languageye' series, and for including several of the visual poems from this work in the online publication.

Thank you to rob mclennan for interviewing me about this book and other work for the *Touch the Donkey* supplement 39 in 2015, and for publishing earlier versions of these poems in the above/ground press chapbook *The Double Bind Dictionary* in 2013.

Thank you to Derek Beaulieu for publishing earlier versions of these poems in the No Press chapbook *False Friends* in 2013.

Thank you to Daniel Zomparelli for including folk art visual poems related to this project in the exhibit *That One Thing You Said* in Vancouver in 2015.

The poem 'Himnusz' is a loose translation of the Hungarian national anthem.

The poem 'Óperencia' translates the opening and closing phrases from the narration of numerous episodes of the animated series *Magyar népmesék*.

Most of the folk art in this book was inspired by *Traditional Hungarian Designs* (Vancouver: 2002), made by Péter Czink and Lorraine Weidman from *Magyar Mustrák* by Géza Kovách (Budapest: Royal University Printer, 1926). My deepest thanks to Péter Czink for the gift of this beautifully rendered work.

The visual poem for the letter *U* was inspired by a piece of embroidery entitled *Embroidered Heart from Kalocsa* from the site Magyar Marketing.

The visual poem for the letters *Cs* and *Gy* were inspired by designs in the book *Magyar díszítmények,* by Várdai Szilárd, self-published in 1910.

The paper dolls on the cover are from *Öltöztess magyar babát!,* György Morvay et. al., 4th edition, Barta & Fiai Co.

Magyarázni was made possible by the generous support of the Alberta Foundation for the Arts.

Helen Hajnoczky's first book, *Poets and Killers: A Life in Advertising* (Invisible Publishing/Snare, 2010), was nominated for Expozine's best English book of the year award. Her chapbook *Bloom and Martyr* was the winner of Kalamalka Press' 2015 John Lent Poetry Prose Award. Her work has appeared in the anthologies *Why Poetry Sucks: Humorous Avant-Garde and Post-Avant English Canadian Poetry* (Insomniac, 2014) and *Ground Rules: 2003–2013* (Chaudiere, 2013), in the magazines *Dreamland, filling Station,* Lemon Hound, *Matrix,* New Poetry, *NōD Magazine, Poetry, Poetry Is Dead, Rampike, Touch the Donkey* and in a variety of chapbooks. She lives in Calgary.

Typeset in Aragon, from Canada Type, and Oneleigh. Oneleigh, designed in 1999 by Toronto's Nick Shinn, has obvious roots in traditional roman serifed types; however, this face takes on an eccentric character of its own due to its unique forms and loose, almost hand-drawn appearance in both display and text settings, making it very lively on the page.

Printed at the old Coach House on bpNichol Lane in Toronto, Ontario, on Zephyr Antique Laid paper, which was manufactured, acid-free, in Saint-Jérôme, Quebec, from second-growth forests. This book was printed with vegetable-based ink on a 1965 Heidelberg KORD offset litho press. Its pages were folded on a Baumfolder, gathered by hand, bound on a Sulby Auto-Minabinda and trimmed on a Polar single-knife cutter.

Edited by Susan Holbrook
Illustrations by Helen Hajnoczky
Designed by Heidi Waechtler
Author photo by Julya Hajnoczky

Coach House Books
80 bpNichol Lane
Toronto ON M5S 3J4
Canada

416 979 2217
800 367 6360

mail@chbooks.com
www.chbooks.com